# RIDICULOUS RHYMES FROM A TO Z

# JOHN WALKER

# RIDICULOUS RHYMES FROM A TO Z

## ILLUSTRATED BY
## DAVID CATROW

A BILL MARTIN BOOK

HENRY HOLT AND COMPANY · NEW YORK

Bill Martin Jr, Ph.D., has devoted his life to the education of young children. Bill Martin Books reflect his philosophy: that children's imaginations are opened up through the play of language, the imagery of illustrations, and the permanent joy of reading books.

Henry Holt and Company, Inc.
*Publishers since* 1866
115 West 18th Street
New York, New York 10011

Henry Holt is a registered trademark of Henry Holt and Company, Inc.

Published in Canada by Fitzhenry & Whiteside Ltd.,
195 Allstate Parkway, Markham, Ontario L3R 4T8.

Library of Congress Cataloging-in-Publication Data
Walker, John. Ridiculous rhymes from A to Z / by John Walker;
illustrated by David Catrow.
"A Bill Martin Book."
Summary: A collection of rhymes, each juxtaposing a variety
of objects beginning with the same letter of the alphabet.
1. Children's poetry, American.   2. Alphabet rhymes.
[1. American poetry.   2. Alphabet.]   I. Catrow, David, ill.   II. Title.
PS3573.A425338R53   1994   811'.54[E]—dc20       95-1850

ISBN 0-8050-1581-7

Printed in the United States of America on acid-free paper. ∞

10  9  8  7  6  5  4  3  2  1

The artist used watercolor on Arches paper to create the illustrations for this book.

To Andrea and Benjamin
—J. W.

To the Bug and the Cricket
—D. C.

A is a letter you use every day,
when acorn and airplane
are words that you say,

and abracadabra,
and ants in the alley,

an ape eating apples,
an aardvark
named
Sally.

Antlers on an angleworm,

that begins with A,

and alphabets
and astronauts are

-OK.

All across Australia
the animals agree,
the admiral's Adam's apple
was a sight to see.

Angels
dressed
in aprons
and anchors
aweigh!

With an  you can say anything
a zillion times a day.

ANYTHING

Beginning with **B**
is a bookful of words

like bald-headed barbers
and blue barking birds,

and **B**'s on the britches
of bowling baboons,
and brides in a bathtub
playing bassoons,

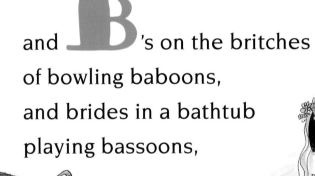

brown bouncing buses
and bees by a bunny,

Buffalo Bill and
his boxing bear, Sonny.

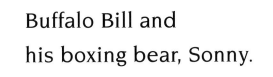

**B** is for banjo,
a barge of bananas,
a bold buckaroo
in a big red bandanna,

a bugle, a baseball,
a bright butterfly,

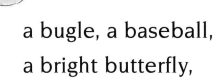

baking up bagels,
and saying bye-bye.

# C

If **C** were not a letter,
then you could hardly say,

that cousin Calvin's canary
caught a cab today,

or cats in cans of carrots,
or crocodile tears,
or cold, cloudy, crummy days,
and days when it clears.

You see, with **c**,
you can carry a crate,
you can color a carp,
or count till it's late.

And call cows in Cleveland, or cause a canoe

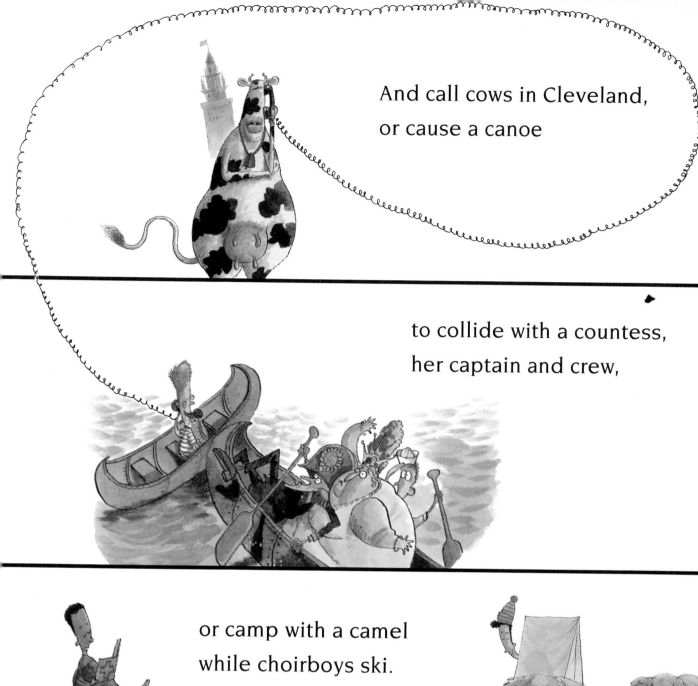

to collide with a countess, her captain and crew,

or camp with a camel while choirboys ski.

But cookie is my favorite word

that starts with a **C**.

# D

Donkey Dan begins with **D**, the disco doctor too,

and when you did,
and when you don't,
and when you say
"I do."

**D**'s for drawing doodads
on my dolly's dirty dress,
while Dalmatians dot
a doghouse
for a damsel
in distress.

Drumsticks from the deli, dewdrops in the dell,
debutantes in diamonds, ding-dong goes the bell.

Dentists drilling
doughnut holes
and diving dinosaurs.

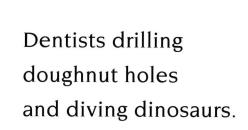

A dozen dazzling diapered dads
come dancing through the door.

**D** is for a dinner with
the duchess and her son.

And **D** is for the dream you
dream when the day is done.

Everything begins with **E**, it's always been that way

like the emperor's new envelopes,
the elk that went astray.

And ermines entertaining elves,
an egg that's over easy,

executives on elephants—
looks like they're getting queasy!

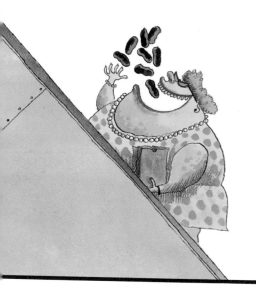

**E**'s for Edna Engilbritson
eating eight éclairs
while riding on the escalator
taking her upstairs.

The elbow room and ear exhibit
are open every day.
An earthworm and the eastern
eel are also on display.

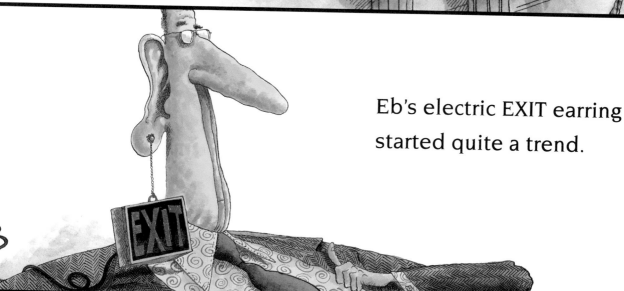

Eb's electric EXIT earring
started quite a trend.

**E** is for exotic and

**E** is for the end.

The famous letter  is for fiddlin' freckled Fred,

 a freezer full of feathered finch, the fuzz under your bed,

frozen feet in February
on frogs who come from France,
a flannel-fashioned farmer
and a fez to match his pants.

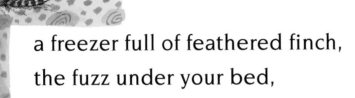

An  could be for fly or flea, or forty flying fish

A force of fighting firemen
flood a flambé dish.

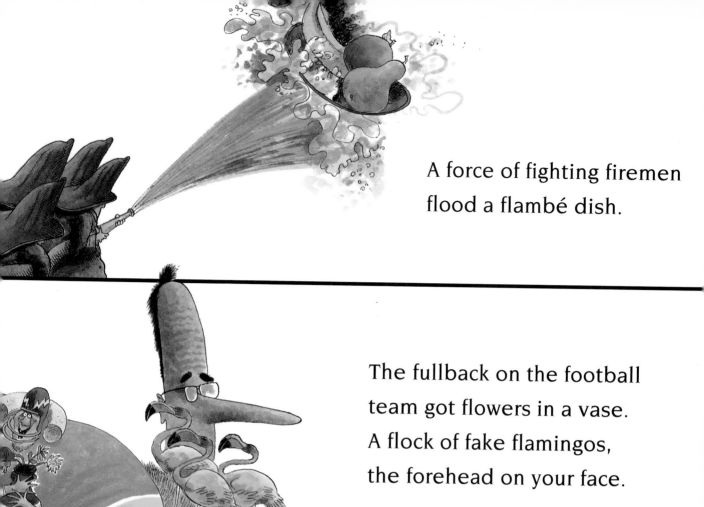

The fullback on the football
team got flowers in a vase.
A flock of fake flamingos,
the forehead on your face.

Your fingers, that begins with
**F**. I have five, don't you?

And I like fudge with frosting,
but sure don't like the flu.

Goody, goody gumdrops,
that begins with **G**,

And gargling gulls
getting gas,
and grandpa's
gray goatee.

And **G** is for Gorilla Gus
and gallons of his glue,

a golden gown
with gloves to match,
a gopher on a gnu.

A goat with great galoshes on,

a goofy goggled goose, gracious gosh and goodness me! The grizzly's on the loose!

A gang of golfing goalies were gathering on the grass, while gorgeous Glen the garbageman drank grape juice from a glass.

A graveyard with a grinning ghost, a giggling girl and guy.

It's getting ghastly, I must go, it's time to say good-bye.

With an
you can say
"Hello, how are you?
Hooray!"

And hogs and
hens with
helmets on,
horses in the
hay,

a huge, huge hippopotamus,
a he-man holds him high,
half a Herb, harmonica,
a handsome hockey guy.

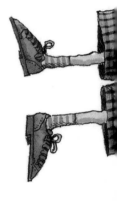

is for a honking horn
and hiking up a hill,

a happy hopping hula girl
and hot dogs on the grill.
Homer-hitting Henry
hanging up some blouses
while hovering in a helicopter
high above the houses.

Hannah and
her hamster
hosing down
their hair.

A hundred hats
with hordes of holes

and **H**s everywhere.

# I

I is for igloo,
Ike is ill,
and ink,

An itty-bitty infant,
she looks so nice in pink.

Immense inflated
inner tubes

and insects on the floor,
ivy on an ice-cream cone,
an Indian at the door.

Inch by inch
an inchworm inches,
crawling up a vine.

An island, that begins
with ,
and so does iodine.

Ida had insomnia, she couldn't get to sleep.

She counted off iguanas
instead of counting sheep.

's for in, but not for out,
and ironing your britches.

An  will do
each time you itch
right where it itches.

# J

Lots of junk begins with **J**, jalopies and a jeep,

And January jack-o'-lanterns that sell for mighty cheap.

And javelins that no one throws, and jeans that just don't fit, The jukebox that played jazzy jazz but then one day just quit.

Or **J** is for a jolly joke by Jim the juggling jock,

or Jaded Jenny
Johnson's jewels,
the biggest on the block.

I saw the joint a-jumpin'
at the Jumping Jamboree
while jogging through the jungle
with a jaguar chasing me.

Jeepers!
Jumbo jelly beans—
each bigger than a jet.

The jar they come in starts

with **J**—

the greatest letter yet!

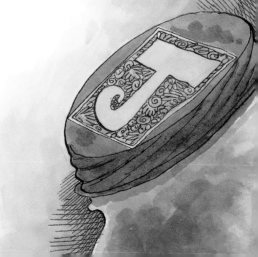

**K**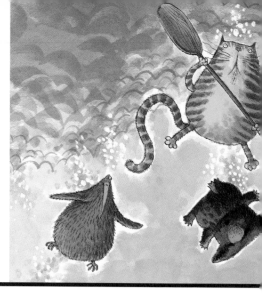

**K** is for
koala bear,
a kiwi,
and a kitty

who kayak down the Klondike
on their way to Kansas City.
Kevin's kin from Kankakee
loved to fly his kite,

but couldn't fly a kumquat
though he tried with all his might.

Even kids begins with **K**,
like kids who play kazoo,
kids who go to kindergarten,
kids who don't go too.

In a far-off kingdom
lived a king
who knew kung fu,

each morning he'd practice
with his boxing kangaroo.
Kettles full of katydids,

that begins with **K**,

and **K** is for the kiss
you give your daddy every day.

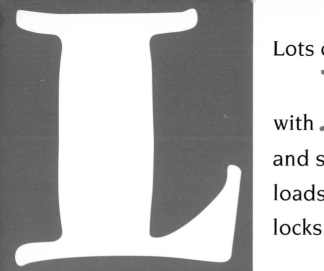

Lots of lemmings start with , and so do loads of locks

and lots of lanky ladies' legs with lumps under their socks.

Her lawyer sings a lullaby to little Linda Lou

at the library of L s, and other letters too. A leopard at a Laundromat, his spots just won't come clean.

And llamas colored lavender
ride in a limousine.

A locker full of leaping lizards,
that begins with  L,
a line of laughing lumberjacks
and laughing loons as well.

Lucky Lindy lifted off.
"To Paris," he commanded.

But without the letter L,
how could he have landed?

# M

**M** is for a
million minnows,
a mustached maitre d',

and midnight
motorcycling
down the
mighty
Mississippi.

Model Millie with the measles,
miles of
merry mice.
Massive,
muscled Marv
eats many melons
by the slice.

A moose from Maine
with mukluks on,

that begins with **M**

and mailmen marching in the mud
as Mounties mimic them.

A meeting of the mumbling men,
they meet each month of May.
Their members murmur messages,
but who knows what they say.

The letter **M**'s for
Milky Way,
mermaids
by the sea,

and moms who are so marvelous—

and **M** is just for me.

**N** is nice for
nibbling noodles,
a nickel bright
and new,

the neighbors
in your
neighborhood,
your name
in neon too.

The number nine begins with **N**,
the number ten does not.

Nine nannies netting nightingales,
nine neckties with a dot.

Normally the nasal nurses
check nostrils on your nose,
but nobody is better
testing nozzles on a hose.

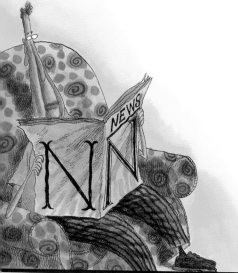

Nathan reads the newspaper
(an **N** on every page).
That Nancy's nasty,
naughty niece
just wouldn't act her age!

When little Nell nods off to nap,
before Mom shuts the light,
she reads Nell nineteen nursery rhymes

and then says,
"Nighty-night".

**O** o is the letter
that comes with a hole.

It's big, fat, and round
and so easy to roll.

O say can you see that
 is for otter,

the fine orthodontist,
and Olive her daughter.

An owl in the oven?
How did he get there?
An orange-colored ostrich
is also rather rare.

The octopus opera,
oh! what a show.
It opens in Oshkosh
and starts with
an .

Oodles of oxen
asleep in the
hay.

And 's for the
older you get every day.

# P

P is for a pair of pigs, a perfect matching set.

The piano-playing porcupine is Peggy's favorite pet.

Picture this, a pretty miss and parachuting pony Plunging in a pool of peas while slicing pepperoni.

Some people that begin with **P** are pirates and police, who ordered pickle pizza and ate up every piece.

Posing for a portrait are the princess and her poodles.

The plumber's good for fixing pipes,
but paints only doodles.
Penguins playing Ping-Pong

and a parrot start with **P**,

who properly, to be polite,
say "please" and "pardon me."

# Q

A  **Q** will do
if you're a duck,
every time
you quack.

You'd quack your way to old Quebec,
and quit when you got back.

A **Q** could be for question,
or it could be for queen.

Or is it for the Quints Quartet
playing on the green?

There was a twin named
Quincy Quinn,
his brother's Quincy too.
They quilted at a quilting bee

a quilt of only .

Quoting from the quarterback,
who's talking to a quail,
"I know you know

the letter **Q**'s
an O that's grown a tail.

**Q** hardly ever stands alone—
the letter U's nearby it.

And you'll never hear the letter **Q**
when everyone is quiet."

Rachel's royal
rhinestone robe,
a rocket to the stars,

repairing the
refrigerator—

all begin with s.
A rhino in a rubber raft
rowing down the Rhine.
A record rainstorm in a room—
I'm glad that it's not mine!

A rat ran up the ranger tower,
then he ran right through it.

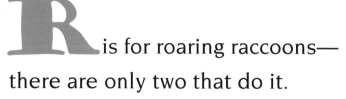 is for roaring raccoons—
there are only two that do it.

A restaurant's
favorite recipe
is rattlesnakes on rice.
The real reindeer
who serve root beer
are also very nice.

The rough and rowdy
rock-'n'-rollin' rabbit's on the air,

and the rooster on the radio

says s are everywhere.

S is for
a squad of
squirrels
surfing down
the stairs,

someone sweeping off the Sphinx,
and seals who swim in pairs.

Sally's on a spotted sofa,
and sitting right beside her,
a squid, a snake, a skunk,
a snail, a scarecrow, and a spider.

Your skeleton begins with **S**,
the skin you're in as well.
A splendid set of silk sneakers,
and socks that seem to smell.

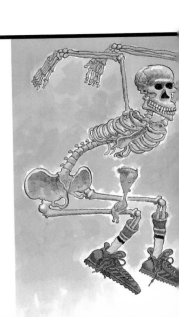

Sixteen singing sailors
on a sinking submarine
soaking in a sink of suds
scrubbing to get clean.

The sun is setting
in the sky,

the stars come out at night.

Shh! I hear the letter
it softly says "Sleep tight."

**T** is for
a ticket on the
twenty-tuba train.

A two-ton toad
who plays trombone
will gladly entertain.

Tammy won't take out the trash—
her mother told her twice.
But her turquoise-tinted toenails
are looking truly nice.

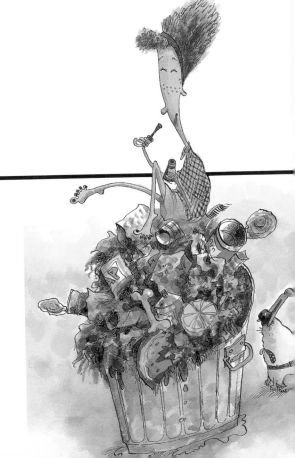

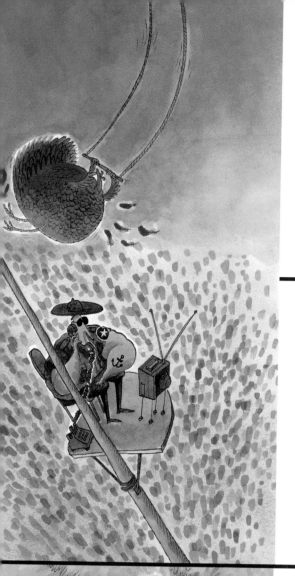

Telephone begins with **T**,
and television too.
The twirling turkeys trapeze tricks
and Trooper Tom's tattoo.

A team of
timid tigers,
some are tiny,
some are tall.

A trillion turtles and their tails—
don't try to count them all.
Twins in towels in a tub—
the tub is in a tree.

In Timbuktu and your town, too,

you'll find the letter **T**.

**U** is for Ulysses
and the underwear
he wears.

He's riding on
a unicycle
trying to get
upstairs.

When you're standing underwater,
did you ever wonder why
if you're under your umbrella,
you simply can't keep dry?

**U** is for the usher
who will lead you to your seat.

It's also for the U-turn
in the middle of the street.
The umpires play the ukuleles
everywhere they go,
but when they ride the unicorns,
it really stops the show.

While traveling
to Uranus once
I saw a UFO.

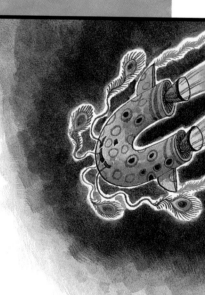

The universe is full of **U**s—
they're everywhere you go.

The letter V's
for voices,
and the voices
seem to say

"There's vitamins
in vegetables,
so eat them every day."

Vanna broke a valued vase
while vacuuming
the hall.

The Vikings play
the Vampires
in a game of
volleyball.

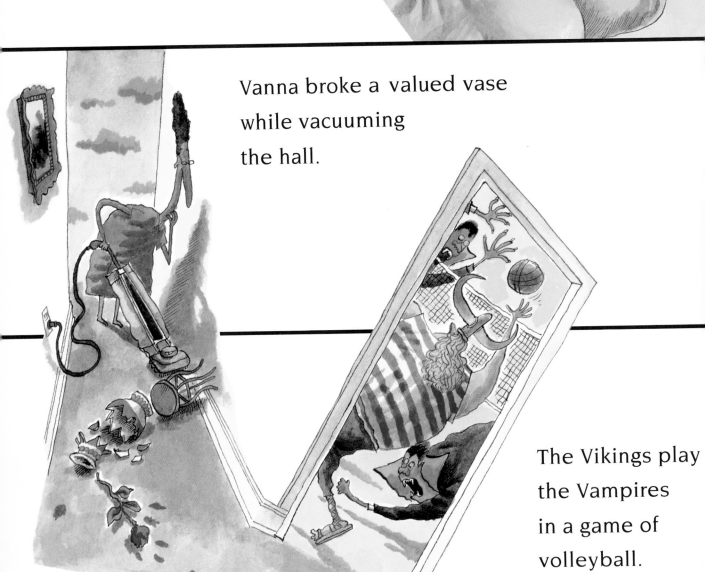

**V** is for the Vultures
and the Violin Revue,
Very Vain Veronica,
and Vaulting Vinny too.

Vacationing on Venus
is the very latest style.
The views are vast and vivid,
but the voyage takes a while.

Volcanos, vines, and vinegar

all begin with **V**.

I'm sending you a valentine—
will you send one to me?

 A 's for
whistling worms
wiggling up
the wall,

a werewolf and
a wicked witch
with warts,
and that's not all.

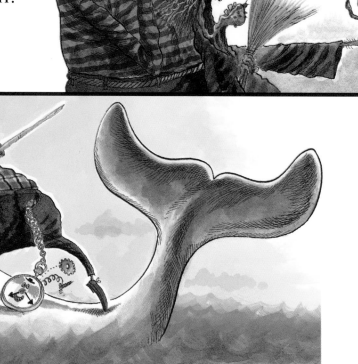

Wally's wacky wind-up watch,
the whiskers on his chin,
walking on a wide white whale,
watching waves come in.

The weatherman who wears a wig begins with  **W**.
He warns the world of wintry winds, and waits on tables too.

Way up in a watchtower, Wesley wonders why a walrus on a watermelon winks as he goes by.

This way to Walla Walla; wait for walk, you should.

With the letter **W** a woodchuck would chuck wood.

 is for X ray,
everyone knows.

Can you make an
by crossing your toes?

A xylophone's for playing tunes.
Xerxes was a king.
When Xerxes played the xylophone,
everyone would sing.

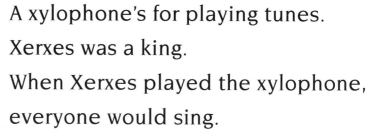 is at the
end of words,
like wax
your sax
and ax.

And  **X** is very useful, too,
for holding up your slacks.

An **X** is found
most everywhere,
from here to Xanadu.
It's braces on big bridges,
and laces on your shoes.

The question
asked in
X-ington,
where all the
**X**s grow:

"How could you play,

without an **X**,
a game of tic-tac-toe?"

# Y

Yawning always starts with Y, and Y's for yodel, too.

If a yak gets in your yard,
do you know what to do?
Yankee Doodle's yo-yo
would go up
but wouldn't go down.

He had to
get it fixed,
which was
why he came
to town.

Try dining at the Y Café
where Ys come on a dish—
yogurt, yellow yolks, and yams,
in any style you wish.

Yurly of the Yukon
used yarn for knitting socks.
The yacht from Yokohama
got stuck upon the rocks.

**Y**'s for yelling
out "Yippee!"
or yelling out
"Yahoo!"

But the best
thing that
a **Y** is for:

a **Y** is
just for you.

**Z** z is for
zing and zoom,
a zephyr fast
and sleek,

zinnias grown by Uncle Zeb,
zucchini grown by Zeke.

I thought I saw in Zanzibar
a zebra at the zoo
whose stripes were not
of black and white,
but were of red and blue.

Zooks!
Zounds!
Zowie!

What a surprise!
A zircon ring for Zelda Z.,
too bad it's twice her size.
A Zamboni writing on the ice—
oh, what can it be?

It zips, it zigs,
and then it zags,
and draws

the letter **Z**.

It's like an I all twisted up,
it sounds just like a bee.
Of all the letters that I know,

the last one is a **Z**.